Book 1

Python Crash Course

By: PG WIZARD BOOKS

&

Book 2

XML Crash Course

By: PG WIZARD BOOKS

Book 1

Python Crash Course

By: PG WIZARD BOOKS

Step By Step Guide To Mastering Python Programming!

Python Crash Course: Step By Step Guide To Mastering Python Programming!

Table of Contents

Introduction

Learning a programming language can be a daunting task for many, but the right guidance can be the differentiator and the ultimate deciding factor as to how well you learn the language. Python is an easy to learn, high-level language which supports both structured and object-oriented programming.

This book aims at making the basic fundamentals of the language clear to the programmers. The dynamics of the language have been explained so as to enable developers to learn fine coding skills. Python has readable codes and an easy syntax thus making it simple to learn. It has automatic memory management system along with a comprehensive library that allows the programmers to write programs in a fewer lines of code as compared to other programming languages like C++ and Java.

Learning Python can be your stepping stone in the field of programming since Python methodologies can be used in a broad range of applications.

Lastly, the book is useful both for beginners who want to master this language and the experienced programmers who wish to revisit the basics or want a manual for reference. We would like to thank you for downloading this book and we hope that the book is valuable for its readers.

Chapter 1: Preamble to Python

Python programming language was created by Guido Rossum in 1989. It is an object-oriented, multi-purpose and interactive scripting language. The language has been designed as highly readable. Python has fewer syntactical constructions and uses English keywords frequently. It is considered as a great language for beginners in the programming field.

Features of Python

1. Python provides rich data types and easier to read syntax as compared to other languages.
2. As compared to other programming languages it allows more run-time flexibility.
3. It is a platform independent scripted language with complete access to operating system API's.
4. Python libraries are cross-platform, thus making them compatible with Windows, MacIntosh and Linux.
5. It supports interactive mode that allows snippets of codes to be tested and debugged interactively.
6. It is a portable language and can run of various hardware platforms with same interface.
7. The Python source code can be easily maintained.
8. It provides support and an enhanced structure for big programs than shell scripting.
9. For building large applications, python can be assembled in to byte-code.
10. Python can be effortlessly incorporated with JAVA , C++, C , COBRA and Active X.
11. It can be used for programming video games, various scientific programs and artificial intelligence algorithms.
12. It has automatic memory management system.

Python is a self-sufficient language and consists of many tools and once the programmer becomes aware of their uses then it becomes an easy task for them. The language makes a solid foundation to branch out and learn other programming languages.

Python Crash Course: Step By Step Guide To Mastering Python
Programming!

Installing and Setting Up Python

Python distribution is available for wide range of platforms. It is easy to install and nowadays many Linux and Unix distributions include the latest version of Python. To download and install Python you can visit http://www.python.org/downloads/ and opt for the desired version. Even though version 3 is the latest but still Python 2 is used widely. Once you have downloaded and installed you need to set up the path. To add the Python directory for a particular session in-

Linux /UNIX –

a) In the csh shell type setenv PATH "$PATH:/usr/local/bin/python" then press Enter.
b) For Linux, in the bash shell, type export ATH= "$PATH:/usr/local/bin/Python" then press Enter.
c) Type PATH="$PATH:/usr/local/bin/Python" in the sh or ksh shell and press Enter.
d) Please note that /usr/local/bin/Python is the path of the Python directory.

Windows-

a) Type path %path%;C:\Python at the command prompt and press Enter.
b) The path of Python directory is C:\Python

Running Python

There are three different ways to start Python. Python can be started from DOS, UNIX or any other system that gives you a shell window or a command-line interpreter. You can right away start coding in the interactive interpreter-

```
C: > python #Windows/ DOS
Or
python% #Unix/Linux
or
$python #Unix/Linux
```

A python script can be executed at command line by invoking the interpreter on your application.

IDE – Integrated Development Environment

You can run Python from GUI (Graphical User Interface) environment as well, provided you have a GUI application on your system that supports Python.

1. IDLE is the very first Unix IDE for Python.
2. For Python, PythonWin is the first Windows interface and is an IDE with a GUI.
3. From the main website the Macintosh version of python along with IDLE and IDE can be downloaded either as BinHex's files or MacBinary.

Make sure the Python environment is set up properly and is working fine so that you can execute your codes easily. (Python - Environment Setup)

Chapter 2: Basic Syntax

In the previous chapter, we learned how to install and set up Python. This chapter we will discuss the Python Syntax. A set of rules that defines how a program will be written and interpreted is called Syntax.

Let's understand various methods of programming

Interactive Mode Programming

At the command prompt type the below mentioned text and press Enter

print "Hello, Python!"

The output in version 2.4.3 will be *Hello,Python!*. Incase you are using the new version then you will have to use parenthesis along with the print statement–

print ("Goodmorning, Python!");

Script mode programming

The execution of script begins and continues till the script the finished upon invoking the interpreter with script parameter. As soon as the script finishes the interpreter will not be active any more. To understand it better take a look at this simple program.

Python files have extension **.py.** Type the source code *print "Hello, Python!"* in a test.pyf file and try to run the program as - *$ python test.py.* It will generate the following output –

Hello, Python!

Now presuming the availability of Python interpreter in /usr/bin directory, run
the program as-

$ chmod +x test.py   # to make the file executable

$ ./test.py

Output will be –

Hello, Python!

Identifies in Python

A name which is used to recognize a variable, class, function, module or other
subject in Python is called as an identifier. An identifier begins with a to z or A to
Z letters or a _ (underscore) which is followed more letters or a zero, digits (0 to
9) and underscores. No punctuation characters like %, $, @ are allowed within
Python identifiers. It is a case dependent language.

    a) Class names begin with uppercase letters and all other identifiers begin
       with a lowercase letter.
    b) An identifier which begins with a single foremost underscore indicates that
       it is private.
    c) An identifier with two leading underscore denotes a strongly private
       identifier.
    d) The identifier is a language-defined special name in case it ends with two
       trailing underscores.

Reserved Words

There are certain reserved words in Python which cannot be used as variable or a
constant or any other identifier name. All reserved words are in lowercase only.

not	exec	and
or	finally	assert
pass	for	break
print	from	class
raise	global	continue
return	if	def
try	import	del
while	in	elif
with	is	else
yield	lambda	except

Lines and Indentation

In Python, to indicate blocks of code for function and class definitions or flow control, there are no braces. The line indentation denotes the block of codes. In the indentation, the number of spaces is variable, but inside the block same amount of indentation should be done for all statements. Therefore, a block is formed by all the unbroken lines which have been indented with same number of spaces.

Multi-Line Statements

A new line in Python typically marks the end of a statement. However, the use of line continuation character (\) is allowed to denote the line should continue. Example –
```
Total = goods_one + \
     goods_two + \
     goods_three + \
```
The line continuation character is not required for statements contained within brackets ( ), [ ] or { }.

Python Crash Course: Step By Step Guide To Mastering Python
Programming!

Quotation

In python, all three quotes (' , " or """) are accepted. These indicate string literals provided the same kind of quote begins and closes the string. To cover the string across multiple lines, triple quotes are used.

Comments

The comment in Python begins with a hash (#) sign that is not within the string literal. After the hash all characters up to the end of the physical line form a part of the comment. However, they are ignored by the Python interpreter.

Blank lines

Blank lines are ignored by Python. These are the lines which have just whitespace, probably with a comment.

Multiple Statements on a Single line

On a single line multiple statements are allowed with a semicolon (;) provided that none of the statement starts a new code block.

Suites

In Python, a single code of block made by a cluster of statements is called as suites. The compound statements like if, else, while, def and class need a suite and a header line. The header lines start with statement (including keyword) and a colon denotes the end. They are trailed by one or more lines that make a suite.

Chapter 3: Python Fundamentals

Now that we know the syntax of Python, it is imperative for programmers to understand the python fundamentals. In other words, we would be discussing the basics on which the Python programming is based.

VARIABLES

A reserved memory location where values are stored is known as a variable. Memory space is allocated by the python interpreter and on the basis of data type of a variable it takes decision on what to store in this reserved memory. Hence, in the variables storing of characters, integers, or decimals is possible by assigning them different data types.

How to assign values to variables?

For assigning values to the variables you need to use the equal (=) sign. The left hand side operand denotes the variable name and the right side operand denotes the stored value inside the variable. Example –

counter = 10   (integer assignment)
miles   = 100   (floating point)
name   = "Tom"   (string)

print counter
print miles
print names

In the above example-10, 100 and Tom are the values assigned to counter, miles and name variables respectively and will give us the result as –
10
100
Tom

Assigning a lone value to numerous variables at the same time is also possible.

Example –
x= y= z= 1

In the above example, with value 1, the integer object is created, and same memory location is assigned to all three variables. Apart from this multiple objects can also be assigned to several variables. Like –

x, y, z = 1, 2, "Tom"

Data types

There are many types of data which are reserved in memory such as; age of a person is defined in numbers, and his address is defined as alphanumeric. To define the operations possible there are several standard data types which are used. We are just writing a brief on them as of now and these will be explained in detail in next chapters .They are –

a) Numbers – As the name suggests numeric values are stored in this data type. Upon assigning a value to them number objects are created. Various numerical types that supported by Python are–
(1) Signed integers (int) e.g. – 2, 4, 44 etc.
(2) Long integers (long), they can be depicted in hexadecimal and octal as well. e.g.- 0122L, -0x19323L etc.
(3) Floating point real values (float) e.g. – 5.0, 2.22, -88.88 etc.
(4) Complex numbers (complex) e.g. – 3e+26j, 45.j etc.

b) Strings –The adjoining set of characters depicted in quotation marks are called strings. Both single and double quotes are allowed in Python. The concatenation operator is represented as plus sign (+) and the repetition operator is represented as (*) asterisk.

c) Lists – These are mainly flexible data types in Python. The items in a list are separated by a comma and are written inside square brackets. The concatenation operator is represented as plus sign (+) and the repetition operator is represented as (*) asterisk.

d) Tuples - It is data type in sequence, similar to lists. A comma separates the number of values contained in tuples and unlike lists they are enclosed in parenthesis. Lists cannot be updated.

e) Dictionary – Dictionaries in Python are hash table types. They function like hashes or associative arrays and consist of key-value pairs. The dictionary keys are typically numbers or strings. The curly braces enclose

14

the dictionaries and by using ([ ]) square brackets values can be accessed
and assigned. For example, to create, add and delete entries in dictionary

```
# make a phone book:
phonebook = {'Tom Halter': 665544, \
'Liza Raymond': 889966, 'Ronald Johnson': 776655, \
'Kim Lee': 443344}

# add the person 'Mathew Peterson' to the phonebook:
phonebook ['Mathew Peterson'] = 99887766

del phonebook ['Kim Lee']
```

OPERATORS

The constructs which can manipulate the value of an operand are known as
operators.

Python operators

1. **Arithmetic**

   These operators execute various arithmetic calculations like addition,
   subtraction, division, multiplication, exponent, %modulus etc. For
   arithmetic calculation, there are various methods in Python like you can
   use the eval function, calculate and declare variable, or call functions.
   Let us take a simple example –
   ```
   a = 4
   b = 5
   print a + b
   ```

   Output will be "9". Similarly other arithmetic operators like division (/),
   multiplication (*), exponent (**) etc. can be used.

2. **Comparison**

   The comparison operator compares the value on either side of the operand
   to determine the relation between them. Various comparison operators are
   (!=, ==, >, <, <=, >=).

Example – we will compare the value of a to the value of b and print the result in true or false. Assume value of a =4 which is smaller than b =5. Now when we print the value as a >b, it actually compares the value of a to b and since it is incorrect, it returns as false. Similarly you can use other comparison operators.

3. Assignment

To assign the value of the right operand to the left operand, we use assignment operators.They are (+, +=, -=, /=, *=, %=, **=, //=). Example-

num1 = 4
num2 =5
print ("Line1 – Value of num1:", num1)
print ("Line2 – Value of num2:", num2)

Output –

('Line1 –Value of num1:',4)
('Line2 – value of num2:', 5

4. Logical

These operators are used for conditional statements which are true or false.
AND, OR and NOT are the logical operators in Python
AND – it returns TRUE if both left and right operands are true.
OR – it returns FALSE if either of the operand is true.
NOT – it returns TRUE if operand is false

Example-
x = true
y = false
print ('x and y is', x and y)
print ('x or y is', x or y)
print ('not x is', not x)

The result will be –
('x and y is', False)

('x or y is', True)
('not x is', False)

5. Membership

Inside a sequence such as strings, lists or tuples membership is checked by these operators. These are of two types (in and not in). These operators give result based on the variable present in specified string or sequence.
Example –
We will check whether value of x=3 and y=7 is available in list or not by using membership operators.

x= 3
y =7
list = [1, 2, 3, 4, 5];

if (x in list):
    print "Line 1 – x is available in the given list"
else:
     print "Line 1 – x is not available in the given list"

if (y not in list):
    print "Line 2 – y is not available in the given list"
else:
    print "Line 2- y is available in the given list"

Result of the above code –

Line 1 – x is available in the given list
Line 2 – y is not available in the given list

6. Identity

Memory locations of two objects are compared by identity operators. They are of two types – is and is not.
is – it returns true if two variables point the same object otherwise false.
is not- it returns false if two variables point the same object, otherwise true.

Example –

x = 10
y = 10

if (x is y):

> *print "x & y SAME identity"*

y = 20

if (x is not y):

> *print "x & y have DIFFERENT identity"*

Following result is generated –
x&y SAME identity
x & y DIFFERENT identity

7. Bitwise

A bitwise operator work on bits and performs bit by bit operation. Python supports the following Bitwise operators - & Binary AND, | Binary OR, ^ Binary XOR, ~Binary Ones Complement, << Binary Left shift and >> Binary Right shift.

Operators Precedence

It determines which operator needs to be evaluated first. Precedence of operators is necessary to avoid ambiguity in values. For example – multiplication has a higher precedence than addition. Following operators are usedin Python – (**, ~+ -, */ % //, + -, & , ^|, >><<, &, <=<>>=, <> == !=, is is not, in not in , not or and)

STATEMENTS

Anticipating the conditions that might occur while executing a program and specifying the actions according to those conditions is called decision making. The decision structures assess numerous expressions which produce TRUE or FALSE as a result. You need to determine which action to take and what statements to execute if the result is TRUE or FALSE otherwise. In Python programming any non-zero and non-null values are assumed as TRUE, and if it is either null or zero then it is assumed as FALSE value.

Following types of decision making statements are provided in Python –

1. **if statements** - it contains a Boolean expression followed by one or more statements.

   A logical expression is used to compare the data and decision is made on the basis of comparison result. If Boolean expression evaluates to TRUE, then the block of statement(s) inside the *if* statement is executed. In case it evaluates FALSE, then the first set of code after the end of *if* statement is executed.

   Syntax –
   if expression:
      statement(s)

2. **if....else statements** – In this an *if* statement is followed by an optional *else* statement.If the conditional expression in the *if* statement resolves to FALSE value or 0, the block of code executes in an else statement.

   Syntax –
   if expression:
      statement(s)
   else:
      statement(s)

3. **elif statement** – It permits you to examine multiple expressions for TRUE and carry out a block of code as soon as one of the condition evaluates to TRUE. They are also optional statements and random number of *elif* statements following an *if* can be there.

   Syntax –
   if expression 1:
      statement(s)
   if expression 2:
      statement(s)
   elif expression3:
      statement(s)
   else:

statement(s)

4. **nested statements** – When you want to examine a different condition
   when a condition works out to be true then you can use *nested if*
   statements. Inside a nested if statement, an *if...elif ... else* inside another
   if...elif..else construct is also possible.

Syntax –
if expression1:
  statement(s)
  if expression2:
    Statement(s)
  elif expression3:
    statement(s)
  else:
    statement(s)
elif expression4:
  statement(s)
else:
  statement(s)

Chapter 4: Learn about Python loops, Strings, Lists, Tuples, and Dictionary

We have already introduced these terms in the previous chapter. Now we will take a look at each one of them in detail so that you can understand their usage in Python programming.

LOOPS

Typically the statements are executed in sequence, but if a situation arises when you are required to execute a block of code many number of times. In Python, a loop statement permits you to execute a statement or a group of statements numerous times. To handle the looping requirement following types of loops are available in Python –

1. **while loop** – this loop repetitively executes a target statement as long as the condition given is true.
   Syntax-
   while expression:
       statement(s)

   Here, it can be a single statement or a block of statements and the condition may be an expression. The loop iterates as long while the condition is true. When the condition becomes false, the program control passes to the line immediately following the loop.

2. **for loop** – these loops have the capability to iterate over items of whichever sequence, like a string or list.
   Syntax-
   for iterating_var in sequence:
       statement(s)

   The sequence which contains an expression is evaluated first and then the first item in a sequence is assigned to the *iterating_var*. After this the statement block is executed. All the items in the list are assigned to *iterating_var*, and the statement(s) block is executed until the entire sequence is exhausted.

3. **Infinite loop**– If a condition never becomes FALSE it becomes an infinite loop. The results in a loop that never ends are called as infinite loops. These loops might be useful in client/server programming where server needs to run continuously for the client programs to communicate with it as and when required.

Using else statements with loops

If an else statement is used with for loop, then the else statement is executed when the loop has exhausted iterating the list. When else is used with a while loop, the else statement is executed when the condition becomes false.

Loop Control Statements

The execution from normal sequence is changed with loop control statements. So when execution leaves a scope, all automatic objects that were created in that scope are destroyed. Listed below are the control statements that are supported by Python –

a) **Break statement** – it ends the current loop statement and transfers execution to the statement immediately following the loop. The break statement can be used in both *for* and *while* loops. Most common use of break statement is when some external condition is triggered requiring a quick exit from loop.
Syntax-
break

b) **Continue statement** – The control is returned to the beginning of the while loop. The continue statements reject all the remaining statements in the current iteration of the loop and moves the control back to the top of the loop. It can be used for both *for* and *while* loops.
Syntax-
continue

c) **Pass statement** – When a statement is required syntactically but you do not want any command or code to execute, we use pass statement. It is a *null* operation and nothing happens on execution.
Syntax –
pass

STRINGS

In python, strings can be created by simply enclosing characters in quotes. The single quotes are treated same as double quotes. It is as easy as assigning value to a variable. Python has a built-in string called as 'str' which has many features. A literal in string can expand into multiple lines but there has to be back slash at the end of each line before the new line is created.

Example –
var 1 = 'Goodmorning World!'
var 2 = ' Python Programming'

How to access values in strings?

A character type is not supported by Python, they are considered as strings of length one, therefore also considered as substring. In order to access substring, the square brackets are used for slicing along with the index or indices.

Example –
var 1 = 'Goodmorning World!'
var 2 = "Python Programming"
print "var1[0]:", var1[0]
print "var2[1:5]:", var2[1:5]

result –
var1[0]: G
var2[1:5]: ytho

Updating Strings

Existing strings can be updated by (re)assigning a variable to another string. The new value can be related to a completely different string altogether or to its previous value.

String operators

There are various string operators, assume variable **a** holds 'Hello' and **b** holds
'World'

Operator	Description	Example
*	Repetition –it prints the character twice.	a*2 will give HelloHello
+	Concatenation- adds value on both sides and gives results	a + b will give Hello World
[:]	Range slice – gives characters from given range.	a[1:4] will give ell
[ ]	Slice – gives characters from given index	a[1]will give e
not in	Membership – if a character does not exist in a given string it returns true	M not in a will give 1
in	Membership – if character exists in the given string it returns true	H in a will give 1
r/R	Raw string- it surpasses actual meaning of escape characters	Print r'\n' prints \n and print R'\n' prints \n
%	Format – does string formatting	Read below

String formatting

The string formatting % operator is exclusive to strings and makes up for the
bunch of having functions from C's printf family.

Example –
print "My name is %s and weight is %d kg!" % ('Alex', 25)

Result –
My name is Alex and weight is 25kg!

Triple Quotes

A triple quote in Python allows the strings to span in multiple lines which include verbatim TABs, NEWLINEs, and many other special characters. The syntax for triple quotes include three consecutive double or single   quotes.

Changing lower and upper case

In Python, you can change the string to upper case from lower case

str = "this is an example";
print "str.capitalize( ):", str.upper( )

Result –
str.capitalize( ): THIS IS AN EXAMPLE

LISTS

In Python, the fundamental data structure is a sequence. All the elements in a sequence are assigned a number; its index or position. In python, there are six built-in types of sequences and most common are tuples and lists.
Lists are the most flexible data type which can be written as a list of values separated by comma between the square brackets. The items in the list may not be of same type.

Example –
list 1 = ['english', 'french', 1996, 2015];
list2 = [1, 2, 3, 4, 5];
list3 = ["x", "y", "z"]

Just like string indices, list indices also start at 0, and list can be concatenated, sliced and so on.

How to access values in lists?

The square brackets are used for slicing along with the indices or index to get a value at the index.

list 1 = ['english', 'french', 1996, 2015];
list2 = [1, 2, 3, 4, 5, 6, 7];
print "list1[0]:", list1[0]

print "list2[1:5]:", list2[1:5]
Result –

list1[0]: English
list2[1:5]: [2, 3, 4, 5]

Updating Lists

Multiple elements or a single element of lists can be updated by giving the slice
on the left-hand side of the assignment operator. It is possible to add elements in
a list by using the append( ) method.

Example –

list = ['english', 'french', 1996, 2015];
print "Value available at index 2:"
print list[2]
list[2] = 2016;
print "New value available at index 2:"
print list[2]

Result –

Value available at index 2:
1996
New value available at index 2:
2016

Deleting elements from list

By using either the remove( ) method if you don't know which element to delete
or del statement if you know exactly which element(s) you are deleting you can
delete a list element.

Example –

list = ['english', 'french', 1996, 2015];

print list1
del list1[2];

print "After deleting value at index 2:"
print list 1

Result-

['english', 'french', 1996, 2015]

After deleting value at index 2:
['english', 'french', 2015]
Similar to Strings, lists also react to * and + operators; they mean repetition and concatenation here as well, except that the outcome is a new list, not a string. As the lists are sequences, slicing and indexing also works in a similar manner as in strings.

Python has some built-in list functions –
1. cmp(list1, list2) – it compares elements in each list
2. max(list) - it returns item from the list with maximum value.
3. len(list) – it gives total strength of the list.
4. min(list)- it returns items from the list with minimum value.
5. List(seq) – it converts tuple into list.

List methods –
1. list.append(obj)- it appends object obj to list
2. list.extend(seq) – it appends the contents of seq to list
3. list.count(obj) – it returns count of how many times obj occurs in list.
4. list.insert(index,obj) – it inserts obj into list at offset index.
5. list.index(obj)- it returns the lowest index in the list that obj appears.
6. list.remove(obj) – it removes object from list
7. list.pop(obj=list[-1])- it removes and returns the last obj from list.
8. list.sort([func]) – sorts objects of list, use compare function if given
9. list.reverse( )- it reverses object of list in place.

TUPLES

The series of unchangeable Python objects are called as tuples. They are sequences similar to lists. Unlike lists, you cannot change tuples and they make use of parentheses, on the other hand square brackets are used in lists. You can create tuples by simply separating values with a comma and optionally these values which are separated by comma can be put inside parentheses.

27

Example –

tup1 = ('english', 'french', 1996, 2015);
tup2 = (1, 2, 3, 4, 5);
tup3= "x", "y", "z";

Two parentheses consisting of nothing; *tup= ( );* denotes an empty tuple.

In order to write tuple that contains single value a comma needs to be included, even though there is barely a single value; *tup1= (45,);*

How to access values in Tuples?

Make use of the square brackets for slicing, besides the index or indices to get the value available at the index.

Example –
tup1 = ('english', 'french', 1996, 2015);
tup2 = (1, 2, 3, 4, 5, 6, 7);

print "tup1[0]:", tup1[0]
print "tup2[1:5]:", tup2[1:5]

result –

tup1[0]: English
tup2[1:5]: [2, 3, 4, 5]

How to update tuples?

Since tuples are unchangeable you cannot change or update the tuple elements values. You can take parts of existing tuple to make new tuples.

Example –

Tup1 = (14, 32.44);
Tup2 = ('xyz', 'abc');

#Below action is not valid for tuples
#tup1[0] =100;

Therefore let's create a new tuple

tup3 = tup1 + tup2;
print tup3

result –

(14, 32.44, 'xyz', 'abc')

<u>Deleting elements in tuples</u>

Individual elements of tuples cannot be removed. However, there is nothing
wrong in positioning together one more tuple with the undesired elements
discarded. In order to completely remove a tuple, just add **del** statement.

Example –

tup = ('english', 'french', 1996, 2015);

print tup
del tup;
print "After deleting tup:"
print tup

Result –

('english', 'french', 1996, 2015)

After deleting tup:
Traceback (most recent call last):
 file "test.py", line 9, in <module>
  print tup;
NameError: name 'tup' is not defined

Please note that an exception is raised because after del tup tuple does not exist.

Similar to strings, tuples react to * and + operators; they denote repetition and concatenation here too, but a new tuple is created as a result and not a string. The indexing and slicing in tuples works in a similar way as it works in strings.

Following are the built-in functions of tuples –

1. cmp(tuple1, tuple2) – it compares the elements in each tuple
2. max(tuple) – it returns item from the tuple with maximum value.
3. len(tuple) – it gives the total length of the tuple.
4. tuple(seq)- it converts a list into a tuple.
5. min(tuple) – it returns item from the tuple with minimum value.

PYTHON DICTIONARY

Dictionary values can be of any kind, but the keys must be of an unchangeable data type such as numbers, strings and tuples.

How to access values in Dictionary?

By using the square brackets along with the key to obtain its value dictionary elements can be accessed.

Example –

dict = {'Name': 'Tom', 'Age': 10, 'Class': 'Fifth'}
print "dict['Name']:", dict['Name']
print "dict['Age']:", dict['Age']

Result –

dict['Name']: Tom
dict['Age']: 10

Properties of Dictionary Keys

a) Per key you cannot have more than one entry, i.e. duplicate key is not allowed. The preceding assignment wins when a duplicate key is encountered.

b) Keys should be unchangeable. By this it means that you may utilize numbers, strings or tuples as dictionary keys but something like ['key'] is not allowed.

Built-in dictionary functions-

1. cmp(dict1,dict2) – compares elements in both
2. str(dict)- produces a printable string
3. len(dict) – gives total length of dictionary
4. type(variable) – returns the type of passed variable.

Built-in dictionary methods-

1. dict.clear( ) – removes all elements of dictionary
2. dict.fromkeys( )- creates a new dictionary with keys from seq and values set to value
3. dic.copy( ) – returns a shallow copy of dictionary
4. dict.get(key, default=None) – returns value or default if key not in dictionary.
5. dict.has_key(key) – returns true if key in dictionary*dict*, otherwise false
6. dict.keys( )- returns list of dictionary dict's keys
7. dict.items( ) – returns a list of *dict's* tuple pairs
8. dict.setfedault(key,default=None) – similar to get, but will set dict[key]= default if *key* is not already in dict.
9. dict.values( )- returns list of dictionary *dict's* values.
10. dict.update( )- adds dictionary *dict2's* key-values pair to *dict*

Chapter 5: Insight into Python Functions, Modules and Classes

FUNCTIONS

A block of code that is organized, reusable, and is used to carry out a single, related action is called as a function. The functions provide better modularity for your application and a high degree of code reusing. Python has many built-in functions but creating your own functions is also possible and these are called as *user-defined* functions.

How to define a Function?

In order to give the necessary functionality you can define a function. Here, are some simple rules for defining a function in Python –

1. A function block begins with the keyword def followed by the function name and parentheses (( )).
2. Any arguments or input parameters must be positioned within these parentheses. Parameters can also be defined within these parentheses.
3. Inside every function the block of code starts with a colon and is indented.
4. The statement return [expression] exits a function, optionally passing back an expression to the caller. The return statement with no arguments is the same as return None.
5. The first statement of a function can be an optional statement; the documentation string of the function or *docstring*.

Syntax –
def functionname (parameters):
  "function_doctsring"
  function_suite
  return [expression]

Parameters, by default have a positional behavior and you need to inform them in the similar order as they were defined.

How to call a function?

By defining a function you only give a name to a function, structures the block of code and specify the parameters that are to be included in the function. Once the basic structure of a function is finalized, you can execute it by calling it from the Python prompt directly or from another function.

Example of function printme( ) is as below –

```
# Function definition is here
def printme(str):
   "This prints a passed string into this function"
   print str
   return;
```

```
# Call the printme function now
printme ("This is first call to user defined function!")
printme ("This is second call to the same function")
```

Output –
This is first call to user defined function!
This is second call to the same function

In Python, all parameters (arguments) are passed by reference. This means what a parameter refers to inside a function, if you change it, the change gets reflected back in the calling function.

Function Arguments

By using following types of arguments you can call a function –
   a) Required arguments –these are the arguments passed to a function in correct positional order. In this the number of arguments in the function call should exactly match with the function definition.
   b) Keyword arguments – These are related to function calls. Once keyword argument is used in a function call, the parameter name identifies the arguments to the caller. This allows for skipping of arguments or places them out of order since the keywords given to match the values with parameters is used by the Python interpreter.
   c) Default arguments –in the function call if a value is not provided for the argument this argument assumes a default value.
   d) Variable-length arguments – While defining a function it may be required to process a function for additional arguments than specified, these are

called as variable-length arguments. Unlike default and required arguments, they are not named in the function definition. The variable name that carries the value of all non-keyword variable arguments an asterisk is placed before it. Tuple will remain empty in case there are no extra arguments specified during a function call.

Scope of Variables

In a program, all variables may not be accessible at all locations. This depends on where you have declared a variable. The portion of the program where you can access a particular identifier is determined by the scope of variables. There are two basic scopes –

a) Global – Variables that are defined outside the function body have a global scope. These can be accessed throughout the program body by all functions.

b) Local – Variables that are defined inside the function body have a local scope. These can be accessed only inside a function in which they are declared.

MODULES

Modules help in organizing the code logically. The code becomes easy to use and understand by grouping the related code into module. A Python object with arbitrarily named attributes that can bind and reference is called module. In simple words, module is a file that consists of Python code. It can define variables, functions, and classes.

Example of simple module support.py -

```
def print_func( par ):
    print " Hi:", par
    return
```

Import Statememt

Any Python source file can be used as a module by executing an import statement in some other Python source file.

Syntax –

import module1[, module2[,. . .moduleN]

From import statement

Specific attributes can be imported from a module into the current namespace with the help of *from import* statements.

Syntax –
from modname import name1[, name2[,. . .nameN]]

From...import * statement

The *from..import*statement* makes the import of all names possible from a module into the current namespace.

*from modname import**

Locating Modules
The module is searched by the Python interpreter in the below mentioned sequence when a module is imported.
   a) Current directory
   b) In case the module isn't found, the Python looks into every directory in the shell variable PYTHONPATH
   c) The default path is checked in Python, if else fails.

The module search path is stored in the system module sys as the **sys.path**variable. This variable contains the current directory, PYTHONPATH, and the installation dependent default.
PYTHONPATH – it is an environment variable, which consists of a list of directories.
Syntax-
For windows -
set PYTHONPATH=c:\python20\lib;

For UNIX-
set PYTHONPATH=/usr/local/lib/python

Namespaces and scoping

A namespace is a dictionary of variable names (keys) and their corresponding
objects (values)
Variable can be accessed in Python in both local and global namespace. In case a
global and local variable has the same name, the global variable is overshadowed
by the local variable. All functions have their own local namespace. The same
scoping rules are followed by classes as ordinary functions. Whether variables are
global or local is a informed guess made by Python. An assumption is made that
any variable is local which has been assigned a value in a function. Therefore, for
assigning a value to a global variable inside a function, the global statement needs
to be used first. The statement *global VarName* tells that VarName is global.
Searching the local namespace for the variable is stopped by Python.

The dir( ) function-

It returns a systematic list of strings consisting of the names defined by a module.
List consists of all the functions, modules and variables that are defined in a
module.

The globals( ) and locals( ) functions-

These functions can be used to return names in the local and local namespaces
depending on the location from where they are called. If from inside a function a
globals( ) is called, it will return all the names that can be globally accessed from
that function. In case locals( ) is called from inside a function, it will return
names that can be locally accessed from that function. The return type for both
the functions is dictionary. So the names can be extracted using the keys( )
function.

The reload( ) function

The code in the top level portion of a module is executed only once when the
module is imported into a script. However, if you want to execute the top level
code again, then use the reload( ) function. A previously imported module is
imported again by this function.

Syntax –

reload(module_name)

In syntax, *module_name* is the name of the module to be reloaded and not the
string consisting of the module name.

CLASSES

As we know that Python is an object-oriented language, therefore using and
creating objects and classes is easy. A class is a user-defined model for an object
that defines a set of attributes that portray any object of the class. The attributes
are the data members and methods, associated via dot notation. Data member is
an instance variable or a class variable that holds data related with a class and its
objects. The instance variable is a variable that is defined inside a method and
belongs to the current instance of a class.

How to create classes?

A new class definition is created by a *class* statement. The name of the class
straight away follows the keyword *class* followed by a colon.

class ClassName:
    'Optional class documentation string'
    class_suite
- A class has a documentation string, which can be accessed via
  ClassName._doc_.
- Each component statement that defines class members, functions and data
  attributes exist in the *class_suite*.

How to create instances of class?

Use class name to call the class and pass in no matter what arguments its *_init_*
method accepts for creating an instance of a class.

How to access attributes?

Dot operator with object need to be used in order to access the object's attributes.

Built-in class attributes

Dot operator can be used to access the built-in attributes–

a) _dict_ - dictionary containing class's namespace
b) _name_ - class name
c) _doc_ - class documentation string or none, if undefined.
d) _bases_ - probably a vacant tuple containing the base classes in the order of their occurrence in the base class list.
e) _module_ - the module name in which class is defined. This attribute in interactive mode is "_main_".

Garbage Collection

In Python, to make the memory space free, objects (class instances or built-in) that are not required are deleted automatically. Garbage collection is a method by which Python from time to time recovers memory blocks that are no longer in use. Python's garbage collector runs while the program is being executed and is triggered when an object's reference count reaches zero. An object's reference count increases when it is positioned in a container (tuple, list or dictionary) or is assigned a new name. The object's reference count decreases when it is deleted with *del,* its reference goes out of scope or it is reassigned. Python automatically collects when an object's reference count reaches zero.

Class inheritance

A pre-existing class can be used for deriving and creating a new class instead of begining from scratch by listing the parent class after the new class name inside parentheses. The attributes of its parent class are inherited by the child class, and these attributes can be used as if they were defined in the child class. Just like their parent class the derived classes can be declared. Though, after the class name a list of base classes to inherit from is given.

Syntax –

class SubClassName (ParentClass1[, ParentClass2,. . .]):
    'Optional class documentation string'
    class_suite (Python - Environment Setup)

Chapter 6: Exception handling

<u>Exception</u>

An event that interrupts the standard flow of the program's instructions at the time of execution is called as an exception. Typically, when such a situation is encountered by a Python script that it cannot handle, it raises an exception. In other words, an exception is a Python object that depicts an error. When an exception is raised in Python script, it either the exception is handled immediately or it is terminated.

<u>How to handle an exception?</u>

In case you find a suspicious code in a program, then the program can be defended by putting that code in a **try:** block. After this include an **except:**statement followed by a block of code which manages the problem as gracefully as possible.

Syntax –

try:
  You do your operations here;
  ....
except Exception I:
  If there is Exception I, then execute this block.
Except Exception II:
  If there is Exception II, then execute this block.
  ....
else:
  If there is no exception then execute this block.

Please note –
- A single try statement can have multiple except statements.
- A generic except clause can also be provided, which manages any exception.
- An else-clause can also be included after except clause(s). If the code in try: block does not raise an exception the code in the else-block is executed.

- A better place for code that does not need the try: block's protection is the else-block.

Except Clause with no exception —all the exceptions that occur are caught by the try-except statement. However, it doesn't make the programmer recognize the root cause of the problem that may occur.

Except clause with multiple exceptions- the same except statement to handle multiple exceptions can be used.

Try-finally clause – The finally: block with try: block can be used. In the finally block you can place any code that must execute, irrespective of the fact that the try-block has raised an exception or not.

Argument of an exception – An argument is a value that gives more information about the problem and an exception can have an argument. You can catch an exception's argument by providing a variable in the except clause.

Raising Exceptions

You can raise exceptions in several ways by using the raise statement.

Syntax –

raise [Exception [, args [, traceback]]]

Here, *argument* is a value for the exception argument and *Exception* is the type of exception. However, argument is optional; if not supplied, the exception argument is None. For example, an exception can be a class, string or an object. Most exceptions that Python core raises are classes, with an argument that is an instance of the class.

In Python, you are allowed to create your own exceptions by deriving classes from the standard built-in exceptions. (Python Exceptions Handeling)

Conclusion

This brings us to the end of this edition of the book. We can easily say that Python is a powerful language and that is the reason why all big companies are looking for programmers who have the knowledge of this dynamic language.

Before we end, let's summarize on what we have learned so far. The book began with basic introduction to Python, its features, how to install and set up. We also understood that Python has fewer syntactical constructs thus making it easy and readable. All Python fundamentals i.e. variables, data types, operators, lists, strings, loops, tuples and dictionary have been covered in the book.

We have also ensured that the concept of function, classes, and modules is covered for a better understanding of the language. The last section on exception handling can be useful in practical application.

To conclude, we can say that once you are clear on the basics of Python you will be able to create almost anything you want.

Thank you once again for downloading this book, hope it has given you a meaningful insightinto Python.

Works Cited

Python - Environment Setup. n.d. 2017.
     <https://www.tutorialspoint.com/python/python_environment.htm>.

Python Exceptions Handeling. n.d. 2017.
     <https://www.tutorialspoint.com/python/python_exceptions.htm>.

Book 2

XML Crash Course

By: PG WIZARD BOOKS

Step by Step Guide To Mastering XML Programming!

Table of Contents

Introduction

When it comes to getting into the world of coding and all the programming that you would like to do, there are many options that you are able to choose from. Some choose to work with options like Java and HTML so that they can create projects online and on web pages that really wow. Others like to go with Python because it is an easy one for beginners to work with. But a great coding language that you can learn to work with and which we are going to discuss inside this guidebook, is the XML coding language.

You will notice as you go through this guidebook that there are some similarities that come up between the XML language and the HTML language. While both of these are similar, there are some differences that come up and we will talk about these inside of this guidebook. We will also spend some time talking about some of the basics of XML, some of the parts that you would want to add into the code to make things easier, how to declare XML documents (which is something optional you are able to do to make the code work a bit better) and even how to work with the different character entities to help make coding easier. These are just a few of the things that we will discuss in order to get you familiar with the XML code so that you can use it on your own.

When you are ready to get started on a new coding language and you want to pick one of the very best that is also easy for beginners to work with, you should learn how to use XML. This guidebook is going to give you the best results to ensure that you will learn everything that you need to know in order to start with the XML language.

Chapter 1: What is XML Programming?

When it comes to learning a new programming language, there are so many choices and it can all seem a bit overwhelming. You want to make sure that you are picking choices that will get you ahead and will make it easier to work on the systems and programs that you want, but with all of the choices that are out there, how are you going to be able to choose the one that is right for you. There are choices for beginners and ones for those who want to be a bit more advanced. There are choices that are great for working on websites while others are good for a specific operating system or for working inside of your business statistics. There really isn't a right or wrong answer, you just need to take the time to look at the different options and find the one that is right for you.

In this guidebook, we are going to take a look at the XML program. This one stands for Extensible Markup Language and it is one of the most talked about programming languages, only second to Java, because of all the great things that you are able to work with. inside of this language, you are able to store, organize, and identify your information with the help of tags. If you have used Java or JavaScript programming in the past, you may have heard about HTML tags, but these two are not quite the same. The XML language is not one that is going to replace HTML later on down the road, but it does introduce some new possibilities because it uses some of the features of HTML.

So, to make this easy, the XML program is going to be software and hardware independent and it is often used in order to carry information. even though the markup that is used will look similar to what you are finding with HTML, you will see that these are two different entities. For example, XML is set up to focus on the data that you are using while HTML is more focused on the appearance of your data. XML is going to describe your data while the HTML is going to display the data when you are done.

To make this work better, let's take a look at a good example of how this will work. Keep in mind that you will need to define some of your own tags because these are not predefined inside of XML. Here is the example:

<note>

```
<to>Jane</to>

<from<John</from>

<heading>Memo</heading>
```
<body>Come to the meeting at ten in the morning tomorrow</body>

</note>

With this example, you are probably able to tell what is going on. The information is there for both the sender as well as the receiver and there are headings and a body message that you will be able to use. But remember that the XML document is basically going to contain the information that you want along with some tags. There are no specific functions that go with it. On its own, XML is going to be pretty useless until you get the right software program in there to turn it into something.

Now basically, you are going to have three characteristics that come with the XML language that you are able to use and you can remember these by thinking about the name of the program. The three characteristics that you can work with include:

Extensible: this means that the XML program is going to allow you the change to characterize your own tags so that they will work with your application. You will also be able to extend the concept of the document, which is usually a file that is going to live on the server. It can also be a piece of data that is temporary and will flow between the various web servers.

Markup: this it eh elements or the tags that are familiar inside of XML. The elements that you are creating in this language will be similar to the ones in HTML, but you will be able to define the elements or tags that you want.

Language: the languages that are used inside of HTML and XML are pretty similar, but there is some more flexibility when using XML. You are able to use it to create and define some other languages rather than just having it set in stone like HTML.

Do I really need to learn how to use XML?

XML Crash Course: Step by Step Guide To Mastering XML Programming!

Many people wonder if it is worth their time to learn how to use XML since it is so similar to what you will find in HTML. You do need XML because there are times when you would like to create and deal with the data. The HTML document is just going to display the information; it is not going to work with it to make it look nicer or anything else.

In addition, working with XML allows you to use different contexts that are not just found on the web, including applications and web services. Any time that you would like to organize your data and send it over to another person, without having to worry about all the displays like you would find with HTML, the XML language is going to be the one to work with.

Downloading the XML language

Before we go any further in this guidebook and learn how to write some codes (as well as some of the other cool things that you are able to do in this language), we are going to need to take some time to get all of this downloaded onto the computer. The XML language is from Microsoft and at the time of this book, the XML Parser 3.0 is the option that we are going to use for our projects.

First, you need to make sure that the operating system and computer are the right kind to run this. To work with the XML Parser 3.0, you will need to have a Windows computer that is Windows 2000, Windows Server 2003, or Windows XP. You can then go to the Microsoft website to find this version, or a newer version, of the XML program an download it to your computer. Read through the prompts that come up on your screen until you get don with the download and it is all installed on your computer. At this point, you are ready to get started with some coding!

Chapter 2: Learning the Basic Syntax of XML

Now that we have the right program on our computer and ready to go, it is time to learn a bit about the syntax of a code in XML. If you learn the basic syntax of your code, it is going to be much easier to write more complex codes later on. Of course, with the options that we are going to talk about in this chapter, we are going to keep things pretty simple to start, but as you learn more about XML, it is pretty easy to add in the other parts that you will want to learn.

Below we are going to write out a basic syntax that you are able to use in this language and then we will take some time to discuss the different parts so that is makes sense for what you are doing. Here is the basic syntax that you can use:

```
<?xmlersio="1.0^)>
<contact-info>
<name>Manny Dunphy</name>
<company>Real Realtor</company>
<phone>(895) 444-1111</phone>
</contact-info>
```

As you can see with this example there are several parts of information that are placed inside. You need to make sure that the right syntax is used and the right symbols, so that the compiler has an idea of what you would like to send. This is a pretty simple option that will have the contact information for this person, Manny Dunphy, who works with Real Realtor as well as their phone number. You can expand this out as much as you would like or keep it this simple.

Remember than when working in XML, we are concentrating on the data, and collecting the data, rather than worrying about how the data is going to look. If you plan on putting this kind of information into a website or you want to make sure that it looks nice, you are going to need to work with the HTML format to make this happen.

Working with XML declarations

When it comes to XML, there are some documents that are going to have declarations and some that will not. If your document is one of them that has the declaration, here is a good example of how you would want to write it all out:

```
<?xmlv version="1.0" encoding="UTF-8"?>
```

For this one, the version is going to be the XML version and the other specific encoding is going to tell the document that you are going to use character encoding for this particular project. As we go through some of the other parts that you are able to work on in this book, you will see some more of the XML declaration and it is going to make a bit more sense to you.

Tags and Elements

Next on the list to work with are the elements and tags. The elements inside of XML are basically going to be the building blocks. They are going to be like a container that will hold many of the different parts of the XML ode, including media objects, attributes, elements, and text. Pretty much any element that comes into the code could be placed into the containers here. Each document is going to contain at least one element, but often there will be more if the code is longer. You can use the scopes in order to delimit using a start or end tag. Here is a good example of how you would write out the syntax for the elements and tags:

```
<element-name attribute1 attribute2>
...content
</element-name>
```

The element name in this example is the name that you would give to the element in this place. The name needs to be the same and matching in the beginning as well as in the ending tags. The attribute1 and attribute 2 are the element attributes that are going to be separated by some white space. You will be able to use the attributes in order to refer to a property of the element and often it is going to be associated with not only a name inside the code, but also with a certain value that you assign.

Writing out a comment inside of XML

There are times when you would like to leave a little comment inside of the code. When it comes to coding, the comments are just messages that the compiler is going to skip over and not read, but which can be useful to you or the other programmers who would like to go through the code. You will find that the syntax for writing out comments inside of XML is going to be the same as doing so in HTML. You will be able to use this syntax in order to write out your comment:

<!—An example of a comment→

Comments will need to all be done in this manner to tell the compiler when to start and stop the comment. When the compiler sees this, it will just skip over to the next part of the code, without causing any delays or issues in the code. You are able to add in as many of these comments as you would like or feel that you need in the code to make things easier, but you should be careful to not add in too many or you will end up with a messy code.

Starting a new line inside of XML

There are times when you will want to get started on a new line in XML. When it comes to doing this in applications of Windows, the new line is going to be done with the carriage return and line feed. On the old MAC systems, the new line is going to be with the carriage return and in Unix it is going to be the line feed. But when you are using XML, this is all going to be done with the line feed. You are able to start a new line in the code when you need to keep things in order and to make it easier to read through the code.

Unlike what you are going to find with HTML, the XML code is going to see white spaces a bit different. While you are able to have several whitespaces in a row on HTML, you will not have this inside of XML. Instead, if you have more than one whitespace in a row, the XML program is going to take these and turn them into just one.

XML Crash Course: Step by Step Guide To Mastering XML Programming!

These are just some of the basics that you are able to use when it comes to working in the XML coding language. They are going to help you to form some of the basics of your code and can come in use later on when you are ready to write out some more complicated codes. Make sure to learn some of these basics to make it easier for code writing later on and to further understand how the XML code will work for you.

Chapter 3: Declaring Inside of XML

We discussed the XML declaration a bit earlier on, but now we are going to break this down a bit in order to help it make more sense for you to use. The XML declaration is going consist of the details that you need to put in order by an XML processor to break down and analyze the document of XML. This is an optional feature that you can choose to either use or not use, however, when you do choose to use it, you will notice that it occurs right at the beginning of the document. Here is the syntax that you can use for XML declaration to make things a bit easier to use.

```
<?xml
        Version="version_nmuber"
        Encoding="encoding_delcaration"
        Standalone="standalone_status"
?>
```

Each of the parameters that you are going to use will have their own name so keep these in line and then an equal sign as well as a value. You are able to set up the numbers, rather than the quotes, to get the code to react in the way that you would like. There are a few rules that you will need to keep in mind when you are declaring inside of XML and these rules include the following:

- If there is a declaration inside of XML, you will need to make sure that you position it as the first line in your document. If you put it somewhere else inside of the document, you are going to run into some issues.
- When working with a declaration inside of XML, you will need to have a version number attribute to help make it work.
- The names and the parameter values that you set are going to be case sensitive, and it is recommended that while working inside of XML you keep the names in the lower case.
- There is a proper order that you are going to use with the parameter name to ensure that the compiler will read it properly. The proper order includes

version, encoding, and then standalone, just like you will see with the example that we gave above.

- You get to choose the quote type that you use, either the single or the double quotes. Just make sure that this stays consistent in the code.
- You will also notice that in this declaration, you will not need to have a closing tag like you do in some of the other coding that you will work with.
- If you are doing an encoding declaration, this is going to be a bit different, but for the rest of the declaration, you will need to keep it all in lower case letters.
- If you find that there are attributes, entities, and elements that are referenced or defined by an external DTD, your standalone is going to equal "no".

So now that we know a few of the rules that go with XML declaration, let's take a look at how you would do this in the code to get a better feel for it. This example is going to have all of the parameters defined for us.

```
<?xml> version='1.0' encoding='iso-8859-1' standalone='no'?>
```

And that is all there is to declaring inside of XML. Any time that you would need to do this inside of your code, you can just use this simple syntax, and then add in the information that you would like inside. This makes it easy for you to get the results that you want and as you can see, this only takes up about a line of code (maybe a little more depending on the declaration that you are using) and then you are all set.

Chapter 4: Working with Character Entities and Comments in XML

We talked about comments and some of the characters that you would use in XML a little bit before, but now we need to take this a step further and start to work on how the comments and the characters are going to work when it is time to actually write the code that you would like. When it comes to working with comments inside of XML, you will notice that they are similar to the comments that you have in HTML. They are basically little notes that are added into the code that will help you and other programmers to understand what is going on in the code, but will have absolutely no effect on how the code will work when it runs. One thing to note when writing out a comment is that you shouldn't try to nest one comment inside of another, because this will just cause a mess and could bring up an error inside of the code. Here is an example of a code that would have a comment in it (take the time to write this in your compiler to get some good practice).

```
<?xml version="1.0" encoding="UTF-8"?>
<!—Test scores are uploaded by grade -→
<class_list>
        <student>
        <name>Lilly</name>
        <grade>B+</grade>
        </student>
        </class_list>
```

Of course, this is a pretty simple example that just has one student and it is likely that you would add in a few more to fill this out but it is a good look at how the comment would be able to work inside of the code. It explains that the test scores were going to be upgraded by the grade that you were using and since we only used one it was not the most important, but if you had a lot of other students in here, it would show up. Remember that you are able to add in as many of these comments as you would like, you just need to be careful about using the right symbols to tell the compiler what you are doing.

Character Entities

The entity of the XML document is going to be the root of the entity tree and it is really the starting point for the processor. It can also be seen as the placeholder. The entities are going to be acknowledged being in the document prolog or in the DTD and they will often work with symbols that are only used for the entities and never for the content inside the code. For example, the < and > symbols are only used for the closing and the opening and the character entities are going to be used to make these visible.

Types of character entities

There are a number of character entities that you will be able to use inside of your code including the following:

Predefined character entities

These character entities are going to be introduced in order to prevent the ambiguity that can come when certain symbols are used. For example, there could be some issues when the (<) and (>) symbols are used along with the angle tags of (<>). The character entities are going to help delimit tags. You are able to use some of the following tags in order to get the right results in your code without showing all of the ambiguity at the same time:

Greater than: &gt

Less than: &lt

Ampersand: &amp

Single quote: &apos

Double quote: &wuot

Numerical character entities

With this entity, we are going to use numbers in order to reference and define the character entity that we want to use. We are able to choose numbers that are in decimal and hexadecimal format. There are lots of numeric references that you are able to use, and sometimes there can be too many for you to remember. The numeric reference is a number that is found in the Unicode character set. The syntax that you are going to be able to use for the decimal number reference inside of XML includes:

&# decimal number.

And then when you would like to use the hexadecimal reference, you would go with the following syntax:

&#x Hexadecimal number

Named character references

Wile the numerical character entities are a great way to get started, remember all of these numbers can be really hard, especially as a beginner who is just getting started with coding. This is why most people are going to use the name character entity instead to make things a little easier. There are a number of different ways that you can name the actions that you want to do inside of your code with the name character references, but here are a few of the examples that you can try:

- Acute: this one is going to refer to a capital A character that will have an acute accent on it.
- Ugrave; this is the name of the small u that has a grave accent.

Character entities and types are important when it comes to working inside of your code. They are going to help you to give the assignments to your work, whether you choose to use the numeric or one of the other choices. You can pick out the one that is right for you to work on your XML code.

Chapter 5: Processing and Encoding Inside Your XML Document

In this chapter, we are going to spend some time working on processing and encoding inside of your document. When you choose to work with processing instructions, you are allowing the documents to contain instructions for every application. You should know that these processes and the instructions are not going to be included in the character data that we talked about in the previous chapter, but they will still need to be able to pass through the application that you are creating.

The processing instructions will allow you to pass on the information that you would like to all of the different applications. You are able to place these in any location of the document that you would like. In fact, you are also able to place them into the prolog, which could include the document type definition or DTD, or at the end of the document as the textual content. The syntax to use in order to make this happen includes:

<?target instructions?>

For this syntax, the target is going to be responsible for recognizing the application from which the instruction comes from. You will be able to place the name of any application that you would like to use to tell the program where the instructions are located to use. And then the part of the instructions is going to be used in order to describe any of the information that you would like the application to process in order to finish it out.

The processing instructions are not used all that often because of the specialties that come with it. But if you do choose to work with these processing instructions, you will use them in order to link your XML document to a style sheet. In order to make this happen, you would need to type out the following type of syntax:

<?xml-stylesheet href= "businessforms.css" type="text/css"?>

These are basically the instructions that your target application is going to process inside of the XML document. With this particular instruction, the browser is going to be able to get the browser to recognize the right target by initiating that XML document and that it should transform it before it is shown. Notice that the first attribute comes out as the type of XSL that you are trying to transform and then the second attribute is going to indicate the location of the type you are transforming.

Working with XML encoding

Now that we have talked a bit about using processing inside of the XML document, it is time to work on the encoding inside of your documents. The process of encoding inside of XML is to convert the Unicode characters that you are trying to use into binary ones. The moment that the processor for XML reads a specific document, it is going to immediately encode the document according to the encoding type that you pick to go with it. There are different types of coding that you are able to use and we are going to look at them a bit more below:

Types of encoding

Inside of the XML code, there are gong to be two types of encoding that you are able to use, the UTF-8 and UTF16. They can both be used in separate ways in the coding that you work on. But if you end up not picking out the encoding that you would like to use with your XML document, the default is going to be the UTF-8. The syntax that you are going to use will depend on the type of encoding that you are using. For the UTF-8, you would use the following syntax:

<?xml version="1.0" encoding="UTF-8" standalone="no"?>

And then the syntax that you would need to use for the UTF-16 encoding would include:

<?xml version="1.0" encoding="UTF-16" standalone="no"?>

As you can see, these are going to be pretty similar, you will just put in the different options that you are able to use for the encoding. You will just need to pick the one that is best for you or choose to leave it blank so that the UTF-8 is going to be picked by default. Here is a good example of using the encoding of UTF-8:

```
<?xml version="1.0" encoding="UTF-8" standalone="no"?>
<contact-info>
        <name>Dunny Bobbins</name>
        <company>Real Realtors</company>
        <phone>(553) 512 1123</phone>
</contact-info>
```

With this example, we are using the UTF-8 encoding, as you are able to see by looking at that part of the code. This means that the 8-bit characters are the ones that you will use. For the most part, you would use this option when you want to have files that are encoded to be smaller because you are just going with 8 bits or smaller. If you don't care as much about the size of the file or you would like to get it to be bigger, the UTF-16 is going to be the option that you should use for your encoding.

And that is all there is to the encoding process. It is simple to use and will ensure that the document is going through the right processes to work properly. You can choose to go with either the UTF-8 or the UTF-16 based on your needs, but most of the time the UTF-8 is the best one to choose to go with and if you don't place an option into the code, you are going to find that the processor will choose to go with the UTF-8 by default.

Chapter 6: Working with the Elements and Tags

Earlier we spent some time talking about the elements and tags inside of the XML document, but we are going to now spend a bit more time on this to see how they actually work inside the code and how you can get them to work for your needs. When you are working inside of the XML program, tags are going to be one of the most vital parts. They are the foundation to your language because they are able to do so many things. You will be able to use them as a method to define the scopes of your elements, insert special instructions, declare settings necessary for parsing environments, and to insert comments. There are several different types of tags that you are able to use in XML and they are categorized by this:

Start tag

The start tag is the one that you will use in order to start all of the elements in XML that are non empty. You would be able to write it out similar to this: <address>

Empty tag

Another type of tag that you are going to use is an empty tag. In between the start tag and the end tag (which we are going to talk about soon), is the text that you are going to write out, or the content, of the code. If your element ends up not having any content, you will find that the tag is considered empty. There are a few ways that you are able to represent the empty elements that you are working with.

To start, if you would like to have an end tag that comes right after your start tag, you would just write it out like this "<hr> </hr>". You are also able to have an element tag that is completely empty such as writing out "<hr />". You are able to use these empty element tags for any of the elements inside of the code that aren't going to contain any content inside of them.

The end tag

In addition to the two types of tags that we have been discussing so far, you can also work with the end tag. This is just as necessary as working with the start tag because it tells the code when that particular part is all done or not. You would have a simple syntax to write out in order to make this happen, including </address>. This is going to be the complement to working with the start tag and you will need to have both of these in place inside of the code. Keep in mind that it will need to have the (/) symbol in front of it in order to prevent confusion and to help end out that part of the card.

Some of the rules for using tags in XML

Sometimes it can be a good idea to know the rules about the tags before you get too far into this process. This will help to speed things up and ensure that you are going to get the best results. Unlike some of the other languages that you will work with inside of coding, XML is going to be considered case sensitive. This basically means that you are going to have to take note and be careful when you are using upper case and lower case letters. The tags that you are creating inside of XML will need to be either all upper case letter or all lower case letters. You will find that a simple mistake in this field is going to give you some bad results, so always make sure to review each of the codes that you will use before finalizing them.

For example, if you typed into the code <address> and then ended it as </Address>, the code is going to have some troubles with these. The XML is going to see them as different because of the capitalization that comes with it, and it will start to treat this code as an erroneous syntax. In order to get this error fixed, you would have to change the ending tag so that it was lower case rather than the upper case that was used.

Another rule that you will need to keep track of when using your tags in XML is that you need to close them properly. For example, if you have a tag that is opened up inside of another element, you will need to make sure that it has been closed before the external element is all closed up.

When it comes to naming the tags that you will use, you need to be careful to get them the right way. For example, make sure that you are doing a good job of picking out the upper case and lower case letters and keeping them consistent when naming things is important. You also are not able to use any form of XML, regardless of the case that you are using, because it is going to confuse the processor and how it should behave. You can add in letters, digits, hyphens, underscores, and periods inside of the names of the elements. However, if you are using punctuation inside of this code, you are only able to use the underscore, hyphen, and period. The names of the elements are not able to have spaces. Outside of these simple rules, you are able to use any name that you would like to name the tags of your code.

Elements that are used in XML

Next on the list to explore are the elements that are inside of XML. The elements are kind of like the building blocks of the language, the part that is going to be built up on the foundation of the tags. These elements are great to work as containers that hold many things such as media objects, elements, attributes, and text and often they are going to hold many of these at once. Any of the documents that you work with inside of XML will have at least one of these elements, but the longer ones will hold more. For empty elements, the scopes will be delimited with the help of an empty element tag, but for the ones that have elements inside of them, the scopes are going to be delimited with the help of a start tag and an end tag.

Writing out the syntax of the element can be pretty easy, but here is a simple example to help you get it started:

<element-name attribute1 attribute2>

Whatever content you would like to add into here.

</element-name>

With the example above, the element name is going to be whatever name you would like to give the element in this case and then the attribute 1 and the attribute 2 are going to be the attributes that you give to your element, and they will be divided up with some white space. The attribute word is going to pretty much define the property of the element. It is going to work by associating the name back to the corresponding value, which is typically going to be a string of characters. When you would like to write out the attribute, you will simply write it out as name="value" and that is it.

When you are working on writing out the name of your element, take the time to see that the name you use in the start tag will be the same as the name that you place into the end tag. In addition, the word name should have an equal sign with it, as well as a string value that is inside of either double quotes or single quotes.

What about the empty element?

So above we were talking about a code that has an element inside of it. But there are times when you will have an empty element. Basically, the empty element is going to be an element that doesn't have content in it. When you are writing the syntax for this one, you would need to use the following format to tell the processor what to do:

If you are trying to create a new document and you will need to use a variety of elements, the following format is going to be the best:

<?xml version = "1.0"?>

<contact-information>

<address category = "home">

<name> Wendy Dawn </name>

<office> My Office </office>

<phone> (632) 246 1234 </phone>

<address/>

</contact-information>

Working with elements and tags inside of the XML document is one of the best things that you are able to do for your code. These are going to help you to get everything in place and they are the foundation and the building blocks that you really need inside of your code. It can take some time to learn the different things that you need inside of these, but when you are able to bring it all together, these are the two parts of the code that you need in order to really get it started the right way.

Chapter 7: Viewers and Editors in XML

Inside of XML, there are several methods that you are able to use in order to view documents. For example, you are able to use a browser in order to view a document, or you can choose to go with a simple text editor. Most of the browsers that are available will support XML, so this shouldn't be a worry. Or you can choose to just click on the files for XML and get them to open up; but remember that this is only going to work if the XML file is a local one. If the file is one that is found on your server, you just need to type in the right URL path into the address bar, just like when you want to open up some of the other files on your browser.

As mentioned, there are many ways that you are able to look and view the XML documents at any time that you would like and the method that you choose is going to be a personal decision. Some of the options include:

XML text editors: there are many text editors that you are able to use and you can make the decision that is right for you. Notepad, TextEdit, and Textpad are great options to work with to create and view documents in XML, but other options will work as well.

Google Chrome: while all browsers are going to work well with XML, this one is really good to work with. there seems to be few problems with using it and it makes it easy to open up the XML code you want to use.

Mozilla Firefox: this one is also a good browser to use, but you do need to first open the code in Google Chrome. To do this, you need to take the file and double click on it in order to see the code displayed in some colorful text. This is a good thing because it makes it easier to read the code. Then at the left portion of the element, you will see a plus and a minus sign. If you click on the plus sign, the code is going to expand but if you click on the minus sign, you will see that the code hides.

Errors in my document

There are times when there will be some errors in your XML documents. If you notice that the code is missing out on certain tags, there are some errors that are going to show up. If there is an error somewhere in the code, you are going to get a message that should contain some information about the error that you are

67

dealing with. sometimes it is something simple such as misspelling a word or using lower case in the start tag and then upper case in the end tag. You will need to double check your code to see what the issue is so that you can make some changes to the code.

Editors in XML

When you are working inside of XML, you are going to need to work with an editor of some sort. The editor is going to be useful to create, as well as make changes, in the document that you are using. There are many different editors that you are bale to use and most of them are free and may even come on your computer already, so this can make things easier. For example, Notepad or Wordpad are two great options that you can use, or you can download a professional editor to use from online. The online editors are a bit more powerful and sometimes beginners like to go with them because they do some of the work, such as close tags that you leave open, check the syntax, and highlight the syntax in color so that it is easier to read. You can make the decision about what kind you would like to use and the features that you think will be the most helpful when you are learning how to code.

Conclusion

Working with a new coding language is something that can take some time and effort. You want to be able to get the most out of the language, but you also don't want to waste your time on something that is too hard to learn and understand. This guidebook is going to take a bit of time to discuss the XML coding language, how to use it and why you would want to learn this particular language.

Inside this guidebook, you are going to learn everything you need in order to do well with the XML code. We are going to start out with some of the basics that come with XML coding, such as what it is and how it varies from HTML (even though both of them are pretty similar) and then move on to some of the special parts that are found inside of your first code so that you can become more familiar with it all. Then we move on how you would declare inside of XML (which is something that is optional and you can choose to do or not) along with working in comments and special characters' amount other topics.

There is so much that you are able to do with the XML code once you take the time to learn this code and what all you can do with it. When you are ready to get started in coding or you are looking for a new code that you can work with, make sure to take some time to look through this guidebook and get the most out of the XML code.